THE
MADISON
STORY

THE MADISON STORY

90 SUCCESSFUL CHURCH GROWTH PROGRAMS OF THE MADISON CHURCH OF CHRIST

GOSPEL ADVOCATE CO.
P.O. Box 150
Nashville, TN 37202

THE MADISON STORY

Copyright © 1987 by Gospel Advocate Co.

Published by Gospel Advocate Co.
P. O. Box 150, Nasville, TN 37202

ISBN 0-89225-296-0

FOREWORD

Jesus said, "It is more blessed to give than to receive." In this spirit, *The Madison Story* is presented. We are happy to share some of the methods we have found successful.

There is no intent to boast. Our accomplishments are by the grace and providence of God! No individual or group could begin to claim credit. The location of our property, the collection of talent, and the spirit of the members must be given much credit for the growth of the congregation.

Summertime brings thousands of tourists to Nashville. They observe our blessings and return home to begin their own programs for retarded children, cottage-type children's home, Tuesday/Thursday school, Bible kindergarten, clothing room, furniture workshop, cottage meetings, extension department, summer Bible camp, meals-on-wheels, Saturday day camp, nursing home visitation, widows' assistance, food room, prison visitation, bus ministry, media ministries, and other activities. *The Madison Story* is written to challenge other congregations to enlarge their program of work and plan greater things for God's Kingdom.

CONTENTS

Puppet Ministry
  The House Next Door
Friends Octet
Teen Marcher
Fellowship
Supervision and Discipline Policy
Young Adult Department
Adult Department

1

HISTORY

In The Beginning . . .

In the sweltering heat, July, 1932, a tent meeting was planned for the hamlet of Madison, Tennessee, a residential community on the northeast edge of Nashville. Members of the thriving Edenwald Church of Christ (Rivergate) felt the need to establish a congregation "more convenient" to some of the members. The meeting was conducted with vigor and enthusiasm, but no congregation resulted.

July, 1934, brought a "brush arbor" meeting to the area. Again, no congregation was produced, but the dream remained.

The season of Thanksgiving became the turning point. Another meeting was held in a private home. With prayer and purpose, they decided to establish a congregation in Madison as soon as a "suitable" meeting place was found.

The search for a building proved to be a challenge. Madison was little more than a country crossroads. Land and space were plenteous, but rental buildings were practically non-existent. Faith moves mountains, and sometimes opens garage doors!

A garage was located in the heart of "downtown" Madison. One month's rent ($15.00) was paid, and the Madison church was on its way.

A door-to-door survey revealed numerous Christians in the area who, because of the "walking distance," were not attending worship. The prospect of a congregation nearby delighted these folks. Publicity of intent was delivered house to house; announcements were made at a nearby school and over WLAC Radio.

A petition was circulated "outlining the purpose of establishing a new congregation, appealing in brotherly love, that they prayerfully do whatever seemed expedient, and that the people might be endowed with the privileges of worship as would be pleasing in the sight of God."

As the big day approached, the hustle and bustle of activity could be heard up and down the main street, Gallatin Road. The rented garage was actually a crude, unattractive 24 × 50 foot room. The women swept and cleaned the greasy floor, washed the dirt caked windows and put the finishing feminine touches on the rough garage. The men built a platform for the pulpit, installed two donated stoves, and wrote on the blackboard: SERVICES WILL BE HELD DECEMBER 2, 1934. Furniture and worship materials were gathered through co-operative efforts. Another congregation brought songbooks and a large table for communion. Other folks donated the Bible stand and a large Bible, and a furniture company laid a rug on the drafty floor. The final act of establishment was the nailing of a plaque symbolizing the spirit of Madison, on the outside of the old garage.

The big day arrived with December dampness and chill, but only on the outside. Inside there was warmth, love, enthusiasm, and hope! It was the beginning of a new era.

It was the beginning of a new era.

One hundred ten people were present on opening day; sixty placed membership, and the contribution was a generous $21.10.

2

THE MODEL

As its model, the Madison church chose the first church of Christ, established in A.D. 33, in the city of Jerusalem. This church had a great program of teaching, a great program of benevolent work, and a great mission program. Since its very first day the Madison church has copied the Jerusalem church and used these major areas of work as its example.

Since its very first day the Madison church has copied the Jerusalem church

---

Educational Program

Daily from house to house, the church in Jerusalem taught the Word of God with great force, power and enthusiasm. With the Jerusalem church as its model, Madison is constantly interested in the improvement of its educational and evangelical programs.

Benevolent Program

The model church has great concern for the less fortunate. Seven men full of faith and the Holy Spirit administered its benevolent program. Considering carefully the teachings of Jesus Christ, it is not surprising that the model church should be so interested in the poor.

Madison has found that unbelievable and wonderful things happen when a 20th century church takes benevolence seriously. A benevolent program so diversified that it requires several men to administer will produce growth and good will. Nothing else softens the hearts of the community so effectively.

Mission Program

The Jerusalem church was intensely interested in preaching the gospel. Urgency is clearly seen in the book of Acts. With this same urgency, Madison uses every means at its disposal to disseminate the gospel of Christ, the power of God unto salvation.

Unity Of The Spirit

The church in Jerusalem kept the unity of the spirit in the bond of peace. The 5,000 member church in Jerusalem had one heart, one soul, and one mind. The benevolent, the evangelistic, and the educational programs were all carried on in this framework.

We have noted with great interest the size of the Jerusalem church. There was no fear of being too large, doing too much, or reaching too many. They loved everyone and wanted everyone to know Jesus. The church cannot grow unless it desires to grow. It cannot grow if it does not love souls.

One More

The goal at Madison is always "one more for Christ". If a church has 20, it should be striving for 21; if it has 200, it should strive for 201; if it has 2,000, then it should aim for 2,001. This is the spirit of the New Testament church. Our Lord taught us to leave the ninety-nine and go after the one.

The Philosophy Of Leadership

The philosophy of the local church is set by its leaders. If the leaders do not believe in growth and progress, the church is doomed to mediocrity.

The philosophy of the Madison church is best summed up in the words of one of its late elders. . . . "Ceiling unlimited!"

The Madison philosophy of progress and growth is in every way consistent with the Word of God. The philosophy is not peace at any price. Principle is placed first.

These questions are asked of any undertaking at Madison: Is it right? Is it scriptural? Will it please the Lord Jesus? Will it advance the cause of Christ? If these questions are answered affirmatively, a course is set and everything possible is done to assure success.

Work

The Madison elders believe there is no substitute for hard work. Laziness is a curse to all Christians. A lazy pulpit means a lazy pew. A lazy eldership means a lazy church and a lazy fellowship. Jesus said, "I must work the works of him that sent me, while it is day: for the night cometh when no man can work." (John 9:4) All must work as if everything depends on each, pray as if everything depends on God, and live as if every day were the last! Abundant reaping demands abundant sowing. Without constant enlargement and improvement of the program of work, the membership cannot and must not expect an increase in the harvest. There is no substitute for honest toil and hard, diligent work. Coupled with faith in God, it is unbeatable.

Dealing With Criticism

Madison determined many years ago not to be afraid of petty criticism. A church that is afraid of criticism cannot receive God's great blessing. Make sure the course is clear and what you do is right. Do not be deterred or slowed by criticism. Don't let dissenters make decisions. Remember you will not always make the right decisions, but you can always make your decisions right.

3

ORGANIZATION

Every phase of work at Madison is organized and under the elders' supervision. They set the policy and exercise the oversight. Deacons and other key people chair committees to carry out the details of every program. This kind of delegation is one of the keys to the success of the Madison Church. These committees are given considerable latitude, room for initiative, creativity, and responsibility within the general guidelines established by the eldership. The leaders are urged to be innovative and inventive.

Using The Facilities

The buildings are used every day and every night. The policy is to keep the emphasis on things spiritual and to spend our energy and money on the teaching of the Bible, helping the less fortunate, and reaching people for Christ. To accomplish these purposes, the auditorium is used twice for Sunday morning worship; 100+ classrooms do the duty of 200 in two Sunday school sessions (allowing 350 teachers to participate). Following the Sunday morning or evening worship, there are often 10 or more group meetings in progress.

This saves thousands of dollars for otherwise impossible mission and benevolent work.

Keep the emphasis on things spiritual and to spend our energy and money on the teaching of the Bible, helping the less fortunate, and reaching people for Christ.

This method has been used successfully for more than 30 years. It was not originated at Madison but copied from other congregations.

Attention to the building and facilities is equally important. The maintenance and housekeeping departments work hard to provide clean, comfortable, and safe surroundings. How tragic it is for a young mother to send her "shining-clean" children into a dirty, dingy, poorly-lit classroom! How discouraging it is for a teacher to spend hours in preparation, only to discover a room with no chairs, no work tables, dirty walls, and lint-laden floors!

We want visitors to feel welcome, comfortable, and safe. The building atmosphere, inside and out, contributes to this important factor. A few dollars spent on paint, flowers, lighting, and a good sound system, makes a difference in attendance.

It is easy to be guilty of having unattractive tract racks, cluttered tables, or musty alcoves. Attention to neatness and detail in little matters, shows interest and accuracy in important matters. The old chimney corner scripture applies well: "Cleanliness is next to Godliness."

It should always be obvious to the public, which portion of the building is accessible during daytime business hours. A simple office sign or arrow direction says "Welcome" to those unfamiliar with the facilities. Should the doors be locked, a nearby sign with office hours, and/or a valid name and telephone number, becomes especially important.

4

EDUCATION

"As the Sunday School goes—so goes the congregation." This philosophy has been practiced at Madison for many years. The church believes with all its heart that the safest, surest way to build a great church is to have a quality educational program. When the Holy Bible is taught properly, other things fall in place. Madison encourages every congregation to put forth the maximum effort to build a great Bible School program!

The church believes with all its heart that the safest, surest way to build a great church is to have a quality educational program.

Every member is urged to attend Bible School. Our students learn from the Word of God how to become a Christian. Growth comes by desiring and receiving the sincere milk of the Word. Temptation is met with the Word of God. Comfort is felt through the Word of God, as one is led by the Word of God. It is indeed "a light unto our feet and a lamp unto our pathway."

The Madison Educational Program is the church's very lifeblood. When the Bible is taught with enthusiasm and excitement, everything else goes, grows and glows! The Benevolent Program is funded, the Mission Program is funded, people are baptized into Christ, Christians are edified, and the entire program marches forward. Madison's goal is every member involved in a Bible class.

When the Bible is taught with enthusiasm and excitement, everything else goes, grows and glows!

Building a quality educational program takes patience, prayer, time, effort, and dedication. Madison Church is a proven example of this philosophy.

As we highlight the work of each Sunday School department, you will see many things the departments have in common.

Almost all departments are supervised by husband-and-wife teams, and each department has an "open house," for parents to view students' work. This promotes cooperation among parents and teachers, and is a great benefit to the child. At an annual appreciation dinner for each department, the elders say "thanks" to the people who use their time and service in teaching the Bible. Each department participates in an annual planning session, enabling everyone to have input toward growth.

The Bible School departments are divided generally by the span of two years. Some congregations have as many as three or four grades to a department. At

Madison, it is held to two. Each department, immersed in the Madison spirit of growth and progress, believes in visitation, solicitation, and motivation.

Babyland And Nursery

"You can't get any closer to God than by holding the hand of the very young and the very old." The younger they are, the better to begin teaching them. The young will not wait. They grow up fast! You cannot begin too young or too early to train a child in the way in which he should go.

"You can't get any closer to God than by holding the hand of the very young and the very old."

Three rooms are designated for infant care: a room for babies under six months, one for babies six to twelve months, and another room for babies twelve to eighteen months.

When you enroll a baby, you gain a father and mother, and sometimes a grandfather and grandmother. A New Testament is given to each baby born in

---

The young will not wait.

---

the congregation and to each baby prospect, blue with name in gold for the boys, and a personalized pink one for the girls. The church loses too many fathers and

25

mothers by failing to give attention to the babies. For example, a young lady attends Sunday School during her youth. She marries and has a baby. She needs God now more than ever, but she uses the baby as an excuse and quits coming to Sunday School. When the church provides for her little one, the excuse is eliminated.

Madison Church uses only mature people in all educational departments. Babyland supervisors have a staff of dedicated teachers and a department secretary. Each room is equipped with furniture geared to the age of the child. The children are taught about Jesus by the time they are able to talk. They are taught songs suitable for their ages.

Babyland does not teach class during the worship hours; however, a special nursery for babies under two is available in that department. In addition, the auditorium has two soundproofed training rooms. These have pews for the entire family. The Sunday morning nursery is operated by mothers who volunteer for approximately one-month intervals.

An active visitation program is conducted by the supervisors and teachers. Their goal is to visit the home of every baby and to express interest in the spiritual growth of both child and parents.

At age four, children are ready for the Pre-school Department, yet have already been in Sunday School for two years and six months.

Early Childhood Department (Ages 4 & 5)

Like all departments in the Bible School, the administration of the Pre-School Department is vested in an office staff composed of supervisors, secretaries, and designated coordinators of special events.

Department details are administered under the direction of supervisors within eldership guidelines. Following the elders' approval, the supervisors select, train, and assist teachers.

All departments are encouraged to have a yearly training series for teachers. Sometimes there are workshops during the week, and occasionally on Wednesday evening. Small classes do not mean small rooms! Some rooms are large, and team teaching is used with great success. The supervisors, administrative staff, and office, assist the teachers in every way to effectively teach Bible facts and attitudes. Bulletin boards are changed monthly to keep the rooms attractive, cheerful, and bright.

Primary Department (1st and 2nd Grades)

Supervisors meet with teachers regularly. The Primary office does almost all detailed work in supervising the entire Primary operation. A close unity among the teachers provides a relaxed and loving center for learning. The enthusiasm of this group is reflected in the beautiful rooms, and the excellent attendance record at all departmental functions. New teachers are given special training. A workshop is conducted when any new literature is presented.

Junior Department (3rd and 4th Grades)

The Junior Department, serving grades three and four, emphasizes responsibility and a strong sense of right and wrong. The Juniors begin to get a clearer picture of sin and become aware of the need for Christ as their Savior.

We strive to instill high ideals in our youth. We encourage their interest in mission work. Eventually, they must accept the responsibilities of the local church. To be successful their priorities must be in order.

Intermediate Department (5th and 6th Grades)

At this age, a concentrated effort is begun to teach boys and girls the fundamentals of faith, what it means to be a Christian, and much about the church and its worship and work. Primary emphasis is placed on knowing Bible facts, great Bible stories and their relationship to daily life.

Boys and girls at this age have the glorious opportunity to attend summer Bible camp! This privilege continues until completion of the ninth grade.

Intermediate supervisors and teachers, on their own initiative and with support of parents, provide get-togethers for those in the department. This promotes good will and gives the new student an opportunity to get acquainted.

Junior High Department (7th and 8th Grades)

No term adequately identifies this age group. They are the most lovable and most neglected adolescents in the Bible School. Ministry to Junior High School students, boys and girls between the ages of twelve and fourteen, is a most important, strategic, and challenging ministry.

Boys' and girls' are separated. The women who teach the girls and the men who teach the boys are carefully selected by the Minister of Education and approved by the elders.

The Junior High Department has dedicated teachers and dynamic supervisors. The students continue to build on the fundamentals established by the Intermediate Department.

The Junior High Department has several entertainment functions each month, given on a freewill basis by the supervisors, teachers, and the ministers and their wives, who make a special effort to provide opportunities for fellowship.

At the end of the school year, an outstanding Junior High boy and girl are selected to receive the Junior Eagle Award, presented during the annual Junior Awards Banquet.

The Junior High students are taught to share. They distribute over 400 fruit baskets to the elderly each year. They also provide toys for needy children. They are taught that the Gospel of Christ is more than words, it is action!

Summer Camp

During the summer, the Junior High students are given two one-week sessions of their own for Camp, during which they receive intensive training in spiritual values by a dedicated faculty. They enjoy wholesome association with others their own age in supervised

---

Camp students are encouraged to continue their education in a Christian college and to plan for an active, useful life for Christ and His church.

---

activities. Camp students are encouraged to continue their education in a Christian college and to plan for an active, useful life for Christ and His church. During camp, boys and girls are separated and carefully taught respectively by men and women.

Junior High boys and girls respond beautifully to a sincere interest and can be readily led toward a wholesome and useful life in the years ahead. The extra effort put in to Junior High boys and girls pays great dividends.

Senior High Department (9th through 12th Grades)

The theme for the youth program is Isaiah 40:31— ". . . they that wait upon the Lord shall renew their strength; they shall mount up with wings as eagles; they shall run, and not be weary; and they shall walk, and not be faint." The American Eagle is the senior department symbol.

Today's young people are intelligent, sincere and humble. They are NOT the church of tomorrow, they are the church of TODAY, and the HOPE of the church tomorrow! In ministering to this age group, it is vital to understand how they think and feel, and to shape the ministries to what they ARE, not what is thought they ought to be. To youth, life is lived a day at a time, an hour at a time, a moment at a time. The language they speak, the way they think, value, and perceive life, is ever changing. Adults must understand and accept them on their terms, while molding their young lives toward mature, spiritual adulthood. For this reason, there are different supervisors for each of grades 9, 10, 11, and 12.

*Today's young people
are NOT the church of tomorrow, they
are the church of TODAY, and the
HOPE of the church tomorrow!*

By teaching Seniors to use Christian principles, we enrich their Christian fellowship and speed their maturity. The program goal is to develop leadership and initiative in the work of the church.

The Junior High and High School classes are divided into three groups: Explorers—grades 7 & 8; Pathfinders—grades 9 & 10; and Navigators—Grades 11 & 12. Each group meets separately, one Wednesday night each month, with the Youth Minister. Plans for future activities are discussed. Prior activities are evaluated. This affords the students a voice in what "to do" and "don't do." As with the Junior High students, this group strives to provide activities that are spiritual as well as social.

Our young people, junior and senior high, are involved in a variety of church programs, for example: puppet ministry, Saturday Samaritans, and Meals on Wheels, explained elsewhere in *The Madison Story*.

The young people are also involved in *Prime Time Players*, a drama group. This group shares the Good News of Jesus Christ through short skits, dramatic readings, and improvisational humor. The experience helps each person learn better conduct for his or her life, based on these demonstrations of Biblical examples and principles.

Puppet Ministry—The House Next Door

The puppet ministry had its beginning in 1972. There was no stage, no equipment, and practically no script—just hand puppets to teach children!

Learning from others, teachers secured patterns and made the first two full-size, "muppet"-style puppets. A simple, small stage was built, and a script was written. The story of God calling Samuel in the temple—"Somebody Called My Name"—was our first "production." The script was taped, and a small cassette player served as the entire sound system.

This program was presented in Vacation Bible School classes and served as the springboard for all future efforts. Eventually we acquired a full staging crew including sound and lighting technicians. The puppeteers were selected from teenagers in the congregation, and were trained in two-hour rehearsals each Monday night.

As the group grew, it was invited to entertain at a variety of functions, including the state fair. New puppets were bought. Costumes were made. A new, folding stage for travel was designed and built. Scripts were written and rehearsed. One of these scripts, titled, "It's Good Enough For Me," was the story of the conversion of the Philippian jailer. It remains one of our favorites.

We provided puppet lessons every two weeks for Sunday school children. Many new scripts were written and recorded, ready to use for years to come.

The House Next Door Puppeteers were now in full force. A new, large, collapsible stage was built, along with more puppets, new costumes, and colored lights to give extra effects. We added technicians. We began conducting workshops in puppet operation, script writing, and puppet construction. We had learned much. Now we could share.

The House Next Door has performed and conducted workshops in several states over the past few years. Our newest building addition includes a theatre incorporating our existing puppet stage, which can still be broken down and packed for road trips. Our lights and sound systems are now built in, and our old equipment is kept packed and ready for trips.

A puppet ministry can be an effective tool in teaching both children and adults. It can stay very simple or grow to any size desired. Above all, a puppet ministry benefits both audience and performer. It has been an excellent opportunity of service for our young people

---

A puppet ministry benefits both audience and performer.

Friends Octet

This group shares the Good News of Jesus Christ in song. They present programs of religious and/or secular songs, for inspiration to others.

Teen Marcher

This publication admonishes the student to a greater life through the Lord and His church.

Fellowship

Supervisors, teachers, ministers, and their wives plan and provide students with opportunities for Christian fellowship. Social and spiritual activities such as devotional talks, Bible studies, youth rallies, skating, bowling, ski trips, special trips, retreats, etc. are planned on a monthly basis. On special occasions, formal banquets are given. Often, buses are chartered for out-of-town trips.

At the end of the school year, an outstanding senior boy and girl are selected to receive the Eagle Award, presented during the annual Senior Awards Banquet. These young people are selected on the basis of Christian character and service. The selection committee is comprised of supervisors, teachers, and youth minister.

Young men and women from this department, along with college age men and women, achieve a special degree of spiritual growth and stature as counselors at summer Bible camp for children grades 4 through 9.

The Senior High students do not have regular summer camp sessions for intensive Bible training. They do, however, have a weekend retreat at Valley View Christian Camp.

Several high school students teach Sunday School classes during one of the Bible Study hours. Additionally, they attend their own class during the other hour. It is important for Senior High boys and girls to meet with their own groups in Bible study. During the summer, they also assist in Vacation Bible School. At Madison, young people are taught to learn, and then taught to teach.

At Madison, young people are taught to learn, and then taught to teach.

One very important goal is to mold young personalities into the image of Jesus Christ. By the time they graduate, they have completed six years of intensive training at the Bible camp, sixteen years of Vacation Bible School, and sixteen years of Sunday School training. The results are reflected in their character and ideals. To God be the glory!

Supervision And Discipline Policy

Supervisors are the key in the operation of an effective Bible school. It is a basis of security for teacher, students, and parents. Capable leaders, usually husband and wife teams, will make wise decisions and constantly strive toward spiritual excellence. The supervisors have always been able to handle all discipline cases. When boys and girls are separated, at the fifth grade level, almost all behavior problems are solved. Classes are kept small to promote participation and individual attention.

Young Adult Department

This department includes adults through age thirty-five. It is divided into several groups, larger than the school-age department classes for several reasons: (1) Sharp, well-trained, and effective teachers are hard to find. (2) It is expensive to provide a great number of small classrooms.

One class is for young professional single men and women. It includes doctors, journalists, accountants, secretaries, nurses, school teachers, salesmen, etc. The class undertakes many worthwhile projects. They provide parties for the children's homes, and visit hospitals regularly.

One young married couples' class collects toys for presentation to underprivileged children. Long hours of work go into this project. On the day set aside, approximately 150 underprivileged children of all races are brought in cars and buses. The toys are distributed, and the young people are encouraged to attend Sunday School.

Most young adult classes designate one night every week for visitation. The teachers have seen the tremendous value of an active and dedicated visitation program.

Adult Department

The Adult Department is very important to Sunday School. A large number of adults in Sunday School means an even greater number of children.

The elders and supervisors have experimented with various types of grading and dividing classes. For those who like small discussion classes, they have been provided. However, the leaders are convinced that the large Sunday School class with a dynamic powerful teacher is essential in reaching the peak of Bible school attendance. Over 1,000 enjoy our Alpha/Omega Sunday School class (two consecutive sections) in the main auditorium. Its teacher is always the best qualified person available.

On Wednesday evenings the same program is followed but with some variety in the subjects offered. Specialty classes are offered: music, personal problems, women's classes, and small discussion groups. The smaller classes are generally changed quarterly. New classes are offered periodically. The purpose is to provide a varied program on Wednesday nights in order to attract and hold the interest of adults. It is a challenging task, but the results are rewarding, and the effort is worth it!

. . . Provide a varied program on Wednesday nights . . . .

Activities of the adult classes vary. Each teacher is free to exercise all the initiative and drive of which he is capable. Classes with active visitation programs grow.

5

SPECIAL DEPARTMENTS

Special educational departments have proven a blessing to many and provide a great source of involvement. Most local congregations can have these departments. Don't be afraid to begin small! The key is to select the right person to lead. The right leadership will enlist talented people and make a success of the special departments.

Little Angels Department

Several years ago, Madison church received a request for a special department for mentally handicapped children. The request stated: "In the sight of God, these children are Little Angels."

"In the sight of God, these children are Little Angels."

Soon, the "Little Angels Class" began meeting each Sunday. Over the years the program has included: midweek class, Vacation Bible School, summer camp, scouting, and Mother's Day Out.

Thanks to a very dedicated staff, this special needs department is appreciated and successful, touching the lives of many families. The Madison church is happy to provide information on this valuable and loving department.

Extension Department ("Shut in, but not shut out")

All members are urged to be a part of the educational program, however there are older people, heart patients, shut-ins, hospital patients, and others who cannot attend. When people cannot meet with the Church, the Church meets with them!

When people cannot meet with the Church, the Church meets with them!

The Extension Department started with two workers. It now has a dedicated faculty of over fifty men and women who travel around the city, visiting some 300 plus each Sunday and sometimes working all day. Many times these caring people spend most of the day getting to all who participate.

These workers attend the early worship and Bible study, and then go to the homes of the shut-ins and hospitalized. The workers include recent converts, as well as experienced men. The qualifications for this department are love, dedicated hearts, and a genuine desire to serve. They take (1) Bibles, (2) a card giving the name and address of the Madison church, and (3) a pocket-size communion set. The elders want those visited to know they are not forgotten. They too, need the spiritual strength that comes from worshipping the Lord! Jesus has said, "Where two or three are gathered together in My name, there will I be in the midst of them."

Great joy comes from active involvement in this work. Many have learned to pray, read the Bible, and comfort the sick.

Letters have been received from people in every walk of life—congressmen, businessmen, laborers, etc.—thanking us for visiting and helping spiritually a mother, father, aged aunt, sister, or child. These workers have helped save many souls and have brought spiritual strength to thousands. Only in heaven will it be known the good these workers are doing! An Extension Department is highly recommended in the educational program of every congregation.

Art Department

Madison provides a place for every talent and avenue of service. Artists are some of our most valued workers.

Madison provides a place for every talent

This department trains artists for each area of our Bible school program. They make classrooms glow with beauty and practical visual aids for teaching the Word of God. Their artistic designs may be seen in congregations worldwide.

The Art Department promotes every good program. Each Bible school department has its own artist. General artists take care of bulletin boards in the hallways of the building. These bulletin boards are used to promote the Vacation Bible School, youth meetings, television ministry, and other programs.

Ladies' Bible Class

Women are encouraged to attend the regular Bible school program, and to help serve in the programs of the church. In addition, there is a weekly ladies' Bible class, taught by efficient and dedicated Christian women. There are two classes; one at the church building, and one for retired ladies, conducted at a nearby apartment building.

Away From Home Department

By the time our young people reach eighteen years of age, a tremendous investment in time has been given him or her. Their souls are valuable and their knowledge of the Bible should be used for the glory of God. The Away From Home Department was established in an effort to remember, keep up with, and encourage those away from home. They receive the weekly church bulletin, letters from old church friends, Bible correspondence courses, and information regarding the church that meets nearest them. They are encouraged to be loyal and faithful to Christ wherever they are.

To Madison's young people in service to the nation, who cannot come home for holidays, the Away From Home Department sends gifts and homemade candy or other tokens of love are donated by individuals. A thread of faith and hope can be kept alive in young men and women away from home for the first time. It can be a real contribution to their spiritual stability.

A thread of faith and hope can be kept alive in young men and women away from home for the first time.

Funeral Singers

Madison is often called upon to provide funeral singers. This is an excellent opportunity to serve families. One of the ladies of the congregation schedules singers from a list of available voices. Though not always the same people, these voices have all worked together and can, upon a moment's notice, provide dignified and meaningful music for a family's most difficult hours. The singers are volunteers and are happy to give of themselves in this service.

6

SELF-SUPPORTING DEPARTMENTS

For the church to grow and be strong, opportunities for teaching must be created. Physical facilities must be constantly used in teaching the Bible. What a waste to have thousands of dollars invested in stone and steel for use four hours weekly! Once a place is provided with facilities to meet and for teaching, we believe we should use it at every opportunity. In addition to the educational opportunities already discussed, there are several other valuable departments as the following which are self-supporting, rather than budgeted items.

Tuesday/Thursday School

The church can be of great help to young families who are struggling to rear children. Many young mothers of pre-school children are on the verge of a nervous breakdown and need a day out. At this stage in family life, there is seldom financial means for providing relief.

Many young mothers of pre-school children are on the verge of a nervous breakdown and need a day out.

The desire to strengthen young families gave birth to the Tuesday/Thursday School program. The school is parallel with the public school, and is practically self-supporting. There is a discount fee to Madison members, because their regular contribution helps provide utilities and building maintenance. Non-members pay a slightly higher fee. There is a registration fee for all. Families unable to pay may participate without charge. This provides every young mother a day of rest.

The Tuesday/Thursday School is operated by a staff of dedicated women. The modest fee pays the teachers a small salary. The money is divided each month with the teachers, after expenses are paid.

One of the great advantages of a one-day school is that additional days can be added when facilities become crowded. (In some states, these matters have legal guidelines.)

Each child brings a lunch, and provides his own pallet for naps. The four and five year-olds have certified teachers who provide Bible training.

It is a thrilling sight to see excited children come into the building, and in the afternoon to see rested and attractive mothers smiling as they pick up their children!

Several hundred preschool children have been enrolled in the Tuesday/Thursday School. It is a thrilling sight to see excited children come into the building, and in the afternoon to see rested and attractive mothers smiling as they pick up their children! This is a great opportunity to teach children. The church is relating to real needs. The church should represent service, love, and care in a community.

Daily Bible Kindergarten

The kindergarten, which is open to the public, offers a quality program with daily Bible lessons. A director, four teachers, and a secretary serve children age 3 to 6. Both school and faculty are state licensed and evaluated annually. A committee oversees implementations of legal requirements, property maintenance, salary scales, employment of teachers and directors, and budgeting. The committee reports to the eldership.

Once each year, a special collection is taken to keep the daily Bible Kindergarten well equipped. Capable families pay a small tuition for each child. The department uses portable classroom buildings which are on church property. There is an adjoining, well-equipped playground.

A program of this kind needs to be flexible to meet the needs of parents. To that end, an extended day is offered with supervision for early arrivals. A separate charge is made for this service.

Special programs are presented for the parents, and graduation is conducted each year. Many of the children in Bible Kindergarten are from families not associated with the church. This is a rich field for evangelism, good will, and service.

This is a rich field for evangelism, good will, and service.

The faculty sets an example in dedication, faith, and love. They go about their work quietly and efficiently, preparing children for school, and training them in the Bible.

Valley View Bible Camp

Nothing is born full-grown. Many Madison programs had a small beginning. When the idea for a Bible camp was advanced, there were no funds, and no property. There was the desire to instill in young hearts the love of the Lord Jesus Christ. Individual donations of money from private sources made possible the renting of a place in the nearby mountains. Tents were purchased. Bible school teachers donated their time, and the first camp was held for three glorious days! Later, an ideal spot was located nearer the church building. One of the Madison members bought the camp and gave it to the church. It contains 62 acres and can accommodate a small group overnight or a large group for extended periods. Madison uses the camp for five weeks each summer and serves many age groups.

A small fee is charged boys and girls who are able to pay. Those who aren't, attend free. Once each year, a special contribution is made, asking the help of those who love young people and would like to invest in this venture. The congregation has never failed.

Valley View Bible Camp is directed by our full-time youth minister and his wife. The facilities are maintained and managed by a committee of deacons. A Madison member, his wife and family, live on the camp site as year-round caretakers.

Staff members are prayerfully selected from the Madison Church college and senior high students.

Many of the counselors attended Valley View Bible Camp as campers. Recently, the staff of 35 counselors totaled 85 years of camp experience!

Campers are taught the Bible, public speaking, sportsmanship, and Christian living. The beauties of nature and the time away from distraction provide a maximum opportunity to influence the young for Christ.

Special Tutoring Service

Madison is fortunate in having a tutorial program benefiting the children in the church's foster care. This program is federally funded through Nashville Public Schools. It serves children from kindergarten through the twelfth grade.

Congregation members who are professional educators, certified by the state of Tennessee, are the instructors in this program.

Session one, during the school year, assists children on Tuesdays and Thursdays after school hours. The second session meets for six weeks in the summer months. The children receive academic reinforcement and have access to numerous enrichment materials.

7

FAMILY LIFE MINISTRY

The *Family Life Ministry* is designed to assist families in reaching their potential.

The American public trends are towards institutional dependency. Responsibilities once clearly accepted as the family's have been relinquished to secondary institutions. Many churches have imitated this secular trend. Inadvertently, church programs have actually promoted resignation of personal and family responsibilities. The Family Life Ministry seeks to facilitate the return of these responsibilities to their appropriate and scriptural places, by encouraging and equipping the Lord's people in their roles as husband, wife, father, mother, child, disciple, etc., through assistance and education.

In spite of our past efforts, we found children who were neglected, mothers who were overwhelmed, fathers at the breaking point, and the elderly who were "leftovers." Many marriage partners were either falling out of love or finding out they were never "in" love. In addition, it seems every family had at least one "hyperactive" child. All good intentions, activities, get togethers, and special projects, were not meeting the needs of this group.

We found children who were neglected, mothers who were overwhelmed, fathers at the breaking point, and the elderly who were "leftovers."

Several new ministries have been specifically designed to meet these needs.

The Youth Ministry serves 500 young people in grades 7-12 in Sunday School, Wednesday night devotional, prime time after Sunday evening worship, retreats, and a host of calendar outings.

A Resource Center is provided for individual self-help by a library system check out of tracts, tapes, and books.

The Singles Ministry meets each Sunday morning at 9:30 a.m. for a light breakfast and class. It is designed for the adults 25 years and above who are single.

The Recreational Ministry is designed for intramural and intermural church athletics for ages nine through adult.

The Women's Ministry provides activities such as: retreats, inspirational days, Bible studies, prayer breakfasts, and classes on becoming better Christians, wives, and mothers.

The Men's Ministry provides activities such as: retreats, inspirational days, Bible studies, prayer breakfasts, and classes on becoming better Christians, husbands, and fathers.

The Counseling Ministry is a team of counselors volunteering to help in special areas, either in group support or on an individual basis. Substance abuse, marriage, premarital counseling, family, spirituality, and self-esteem are a few of the various needs.

The Personal Enrichment Program provides film series, retreats, and classes to build better lives for the Lord and fellow man.

The Substance Abuse Program is designed for individuals and families of individuals who are struggling with chemical dependencies. Seminars, classes, and support groups are available.

The Scouting Ministry is the organization of scout troops under the direction of Christian scout leaders in the congregation.

The Family Enrichment Ministry is a combination of films, retreats, classes, and counseling provisions for various needs and timely topics for the family.

39'ers Program

The 39'ers Program is designed for approximately 1,000 members who are 60-and-above years of age ("39 and holding").

Recent statistics show persons 65 or older make up about twelve percent (28,000,000) of the U.S. population, and are increasing faster than any other age group in America.

Realizing the impact of these statistics, the Madison Church determined to meet the need. This age group was invited to join hands and hearts in Christian fellowship and service.

The program is active March through December, thus avoiding the bad winter weather. The 39'ers meet each month for a covered dish dinner, business session, and an assortment of entertainment such as films, drama groups, choral groups, etc. Each spring, the young people of the church host a kick-off banquet. They provide entertainment. A king and queen are selected, and the evening is capped with door prizes.

No dues are involved. Special contributions are sometimes received for specific projects. All entertainment is volunteered and food is furnished by the members. Transportation from local retirement centers is provided by the church buses.

Programs also include short trips, mid-week trips, and some week-end excursions. As a group, travel is economical. The trips strengthen friendships by building memories of happy times together.

The short trips include: shopping centers, park and picnic outings, arts and crafts festivals, museums, historic sites, state fairs, and boat trips.

Longer trips may include national parks and tourist attractions such as outdoor dramas.

The program provides many opportunities for the "39'ers" members and keeps them in touch with one another's needs in sorrow and in joy.

The program provides many opportunities for the "39'ers" members and keeps them in touch with one another's needs in sorrow and in joy.

8

USING THE MEDIA

The Gospel must be communicated. Madison strives to make good use of print and broadcast.

Members are encouraged to receive Christian publications in their home, but in many cases, unless these magazines are sent by the church, those who need them most will never receive them. Every congregation should use Christian publications to strengthen the home.

Church Bulletin

Madison publishes a weekly bulletin to promote its local program. *The Madison Marcher* never contains irrelevant material, and never criticizes the work of others. The *Marcher* keeps the church family informed. It is not unusual to see scores of names in the bulletin, including the names of the sick, the bereaved, new babies, and especially names and addresses of new converts. It blazes with enthusiasm for the local program and the people involved!

The *Marcher* is mailed to every family. It reminds them of the coming Lord's Day. Handing out the bulletin on Sunday morning is less effective. It fails to reach those who need it most. A bulletin worth printing is worth mailing!

A bulletin worth printing is worth mailing!

Print Shop

Madison has an efficient and well-equipped print shop. It serves the entire church program. It is capably supervised by a retired printing professional and a staff of volunteer workers. In addition to The Marcher, much of the educational material is printed in the church print shop.

Direct Mail

Several brochures are mailed each year to every family in the community. The church goal is to reach 15,000 to 50,000 within the area of the building. Because these brochures are complicated, multi-color productions, the use of outside shops is required to do the work. Material mailed to the community should be the very finest that can be provided! These brochures are carefully worded in order to build good will for the church and to reach the lost. Example: "If you are not now enrolled in a Sunday School class, here is a special invitation to you!"

Editorial Board

Throughout the year, the Madison church produces a number of booklets, Bible correspondence courses, promotional handouts, and various church related items.

The elders believe anything representing the church should be as error free as possible and of the highest quality.

To that end, an editorial board and policy have been formed. All material published under the banner of the Madison church, is to proceed through the flow chart governed by this board. Each item may be proofread 6 to 10 times by a variety of readers representing different disciplines. They include Bible scholars, historians, grammarians, lay-out designers, printers, advertising personnel, and others as the job demands.

Once proofing is completed, the author re-examines the material to be sure the original intent and message is intact. Once confirmed, the document is then submitted to the elders for final approval before printing.

Library

Madison's library is operated by one of its retired preachers and his wife.

Each month, new books are added. They are catalogued by the Dewey Decimal System. The library is open before and after each assembly of the church, and at advertised weekday hours. All Bible school teachers, personal workers, and members are urged to use it. A library is not easy to build, but is worth the effort!

Periodically, the library has open house and invites the entire congregation to browse. The church bulletin carries announcements of new books or books of interest on individual subjects.

Advertising

Madison believes in advertising. A church with no sign is a sign of not much church!

A church with no sign is a sign of not much church!

Madison's changeable marquee is one of its most valuable assets. It is read each day by thousands of motorists. The message is kept positive and humorous. It promotes our worship, Bible study, community programs, and good will for the church.

Madison's advertising program includes weekly newspaper ads, occasional billboards, convenience items like maps and key chains, and for the children, balloons and other toys. Some have criticized the toys as a waste of the Lord's money. The church concluded long ago that a child was much more likely to read a balloon than a newspaper ad!

The use of radio and TV, frequently in "spot form" is an excellent opportunity to reach hundreds and even thousands. Well-placed 30-second radio spots can deliver a positive message to a specific audience. Occasionally, several sister congregations join together in creating an area-wide advertising campaign.

Madison also believes strongly in the public relations form of advertising. Mailing lists are kept of all local news media, and they are informed regularly of church activities. Relationships with media people have to be cultivated. We recommend an occasional personal visit, a well-timed thank-you, and a conscientious effort to provide information by their professional standards. The more we accommodate them, the more they'll help us, often without charge.

Madison also keeps a computerized list of brotherhood publications for occasional national press releases.

One of the most memorable and successful advertising efforts has been the "historic medallion." On each occasion of record attendance, new building openings, or other historic assembly, a medallion is presented those in attendance commemorating the event. Members enjoy collecting these and many have them mounted for preservation and family treasures. The value here is that the children see the high esteem in which parents and grandparents hold the Madison church.

The entire advertising program is co-ordinated through Christian Productions, Inc., the "in house" agency, thereby saving 15 percent or more on space and time "buys." Ideas for advertising campaigns are generated in "brainstorming" sessions by the departments and committees involved. The full time staff also contributes to the "advertising pool."

It is important that the church have a familiar logo and strong local image. A planned program of advertising and public relations makes this possible.

Audio/Video Tape Ministry

Christian Productions also supervises the audio/video tape ministry. Every public worship assembly is recorded. Almost every adult class is recorded. These tapes are made available to the public. This is a valuable service to the members and to others who are interested in the Bible school program.

Spaced repetition is a proven effective way to learn. Listen, listen, and listen some more. When the audiences enjoy and benefit from a lesson, they have the option of hearing or seeing that lesson over and over again, thus reinforcing what they have learned. Many of the classroom series are packaged in album form. These attractive hard plastic cases contain each lesson presented in the series and make excellent gifts for friends and family away from home, or for those who might not be members of the Lord's church. The tapes are priced reasonably, while at the same time making the program self-supporting. Orders come in for classes, sermons, special singings, and historical events; and not only from Madison members, but Christians nationwide who are interested in hearing the exceptional teaching staff.

A lesson worth hearing is worth hearing again! Congregations everywhere are urged to record their sermons and classes. If you record a lesson and no one wants a copy, you've lost nothing. If you don't record a lesson and someone wants a copy, you've lost everything!

Tapes are catalogued and advertised in many publications. This valuable service is performed entirely by volunteers, under the direction of the Christian Productions.

Bible Correspondence School

One of our most effective departments is the Bible Correspondence School. It is operated as an adjunct to our television ministry, and is served by many fine volunteer workers.

Many of the courses have been written and published by brotherhood writers. Qualified writers at Madison also develop courses. We endeavor to keep the lessons interesting and biblical. They are produced uniformly for ease of grading and record keeping. There are specialized lessons for children and for prisoners.

When a new Bible correspondence course is created, every member of the congregation is urged to take the course. Bible school teachers especially are urged to complete these lessons and improve their knowledge of the Word of God.

There are students from almost every state and many foreign countries. Records are computerized for easy reference.

A group of several studies comprises a level of learning achievement. As the student completes each level, a beautiful certificate is awarded to acknowledge the accomplishment, and a local congregation is notified for follow up work. Students are urged to complete all levels of study.

Audio Booth

The 3500 seat auditorium was patterned after the Ryman Auditorium (former home of the Grand Ole Opry), and provides excellent visibility and acoustics.

In the auditorium, and in all large classrooms, sound equipment is used. This involves a number of microphones, many of them cordless. This requires knowledge of technical equipment and attention to detail. The audio booth is manned by qualified volunteers (another advantage enjoyed by larger congregations), who monitor the sound level and record each lesson. The tapes are forwarded to the audio/video center for duplication and distribution. For special occasions such as weddings, etc., those using the auditorium are asked to make special arrangements with the audio team.

Television Ministry

Since the early days of television, Madison has been able to use this marvelous medium for the glory of God and the good of mankind. The first effort was a five minute "sign-on, sign-off" devotional program called, "Five Golden Minutes." Later the church produced "Know Your Bible," an award-winning local program, using a quiz-show format. This program ran approximately ten years.

On the surface, television seems expensive, but cost divided by the number of potential viewers makes the investment actually cheaper than distributing tracts. The good news is that the price is actually becoming more competitive!

One of the most extensive efforts is the Amazing Grace Bible Class television ministry, taped in the auditorium each Sunday evening by a professional production company, and distributed by satellite and tape syndication. Amazing Grace has been seen on more than one hundred U.S. television stations, and around the world via the Armed Forces Radio and Television Network. The plan is to eventually operate our own professional equipment.

To convert a soul to Christ, there must first be an awareness, then interest, personal contact, and in-depth study, before a decision is made. Mass media may be the world's finest method for establishing awareness and interest, but it has its limitations. It will not take the place of personal contact and "in-depth" study.

Millions need to know of the undenominational church of Christ. Mass media can accomplish that. Amazing Grace's positive note creates a good image.

Some do not understand this "soft sell" approach, but the success of others has shown Madison that the positive approach is the proper use of mass media.

Millions need to know of the undenominational church of Christ.

The production cost of Amazing Grace Bible Class is paid from a collection taken each Sunday evening. The program is furnished free of charge to any congregation or group of congregations who would like to air it in their local market. Congregations who want Amazing Grace in their locality should contact Christian Productions, Inc., 106 Gallatin Road N., Madison, TN 37115. Immediate investigation without cost will be made and details reported.

The Mission Committee has supported Amazing Grace in several areas. The program also has the support of television class members who want to promote Amazing Grace in places where the church is not widely known.

It is recommended that the local preacher appear on the air following the broadcast, giving the name and address of the church and times of services.

Amazing Grace prints a quarterly magazine featuring news of the class and listing new stations carrying the program as they are added. The Madison Church also offer free Bible correspondence courses especially prepared for the Amazing Grace TV Bible Class.

We invite Nashville area visitors to attend the taping at 6:30 Sunday evening! To see the crowd and sing with 3,000 will be a memorable and inspirational experience.

There are numerous other ways to use this exciting electronic marvel. Every church should explore the teaching possibilities of television!

Telephone Answering Service

We believe no church phone should go unanswered! Many of the calls are for help, advice, prayer, or emergency assistance. A church ready and anxious to serve needs to be a church that answers its phone! Where or when it is not possible to have an operator on duty, an automatic answering machine is very valuable.

We believe no church phone should go unanswered!

We use a clear and cheerful voice on the answering machine. We advise callers that the church is ready to serve, and will respond quickly if the caller will leave his name and number. On weekends, we have an extended message advising the times of Bible study and worship. This is most helpful for travelers. It is also helpful for the message to include an emergency number. In addition, we use the type of machine that can be tripped from remote locations and give the elders and ministers easy access to messages.

Telephone answering machines are not expensive, and this modern technology needs to be used to the glory of God!

Sunday mornings and evenings, the church telephone is manned one hour before assemblies, and during assemblies, for the convenience of those who might need to call. Volunteers rotate this duty.

Telephone Answering Service

We believe no church phone should go unanswered! Many of the calls are for help, advice, prayer, or emergency assistance. A church ready and anxious to serve needs to be a church that answers its phone! Where or when it is not possible to have an operator on duty, an automatic answering machine is very valuable.

9

MISSION PROGRAM

Our Lord, in the Great Commission, said, "Go into all the world and preach the gospel to every creature." GO is a key word!

In the parable of the Great Supper, Jesus teaches all to go into the highways and hedges and compel them to come in. The congregation that gets all excited about "going" away from home, but will not "go" across the street, is not likely to grow!

The congregation that gets all excited about "going" away from home, but will not "go" across the street, is not likely to grow!

Frequently we do not open our hearts to men and women of all races, colors or economic status. Too often congregations are established for the well-to-do. The church must go into the highways and byways and open its heart to the poor, the lowly, and the downtrodden.

Often, "when the poor and the lowly move in—we move out to the rich suburbs." As a result, the inner city in many places is now churchless, leaderless, and Godless. Until the local church learns to go into its own communities and open its heart to all men, it will be preaching one thing and practicing another. Today's bright, sharp, young minds will see the hypocrisy and inconsistency. Madison has attempted to deal positively with this problem.

Missionaries Supported By Madison

One of Madison's major thrusts is its mission program. The church is honored and privileged to preach in this land, as well as in others. Worldwide mission efforts strengthen the Lord's work at home and abroad.

Madison gives its missionaries more than full-time monetary support. They are given our prayers, counsel, care, and concern. A congregation which knows its missionary personally, feels a greater interest in mission work. Occasionally, prospective missionaries are brought to Madison to live and work with the congregation before entering a mission field. If the missionaries cannot do the job at home, they are not likely to do the job away from home.

If the missionaries cannot do the job at home, they are not likely to do the job away from home.

The church needs young people to be mission minded. Having the missionaries at Madison for a while, gives the students an opportunity to know them personally. The Junior high department periodically conducts a three month study featuring a missionary and country each week. The students are acquainted with the background, culture, customs, and religions of foreign lands where Madison has an interest in mission work. The goal is to familiarize students at a young age with mission work so that it will become a lifetime endeavor. Several departments and Bible classes "adopt" a missionary. They write and encourage him.

The mission committee is charged, by the elders, with the responsibility of caring for the specific needs of the individual missionaries and their families. The committee diligently maintains communication with each missionary family, and keeps them informed of all Madison plans and policies involving mission programs and personalities.

Missionaries are encouraged to select a field and give their lives to it, or at least stay until there is a strong, self-supporting congregation. Madison would like to see a great church in every city on earth, one that is united and strong, where the poor, the lowly, and men of all ages, races, and ethnic groups are united in a great work for Christ!

It is recommended that, if a congregation can, it fully support a preacher and stay with him and the work until it can stand alone. Missionaries who have one source of support and leadership are the ones who excel. Madison families are encouraged to visit missionaries and give them moral support.

It is disappointing when missionaries do not remain in one mission area long enough to build a self-supporting church. It sometimes takes two or three consecutive workers at one place before the mission point becomes self-supporting. There is a continuing search for the right missionaries for the right places.

Bus Ministry

The bus evangelists are usually husband-and-wife teams.

One of the keys to bus ministry is visitation. It is essential for bus ministers to visit on Saturday in order to bring them in on Sunday.

The Madison Church purposely started small with the bus ministry. The reason is twofold: (1) there was a limited space; and (2) the elders were anxious for these boys and girls who came in through the bus ministry to receive quality education in the Bible school. Of course, the Lord will provide, and there are hopes that some day there will be dozens of buses and adequate facilities to take care of many hundreds of boys and girls.

Great patience, prayer, and wisdom are essential in this type of mission work. But it has proved successful in many congregations as well as our own.

Prison Ministry

Penal institutions are a great field of mission possibilities in any large city. One of the deacons directs the Prison Ministry. He is assisted by his wife and a group of volunteers. Bible classes and worship are conducted at the State Penitentiaries for men and women, the County Workhouse, and the Metropolitan Jail. Madison assists in supporting an area co-ordinator for this work. They are also involved in the Federal Prison Outreach ministry on a national level. This program is multi-lingual. Madison supplies literature and financing for the program.

Workers are reminded that they are not judge and jury. It is not the business of the church to get anyone out of prison! It is the business of the church to bring the saving message of Jesus Christ to the hearts of men and women.

Madison workers have accepted this philosophy. They respect the rules of the prison. When persons we have taught are released, everything possible is done to assist them. They are welcomed into the church fellowship or introduced to a local congregation in their area. They are assisted in getting a job, and offered acceptance and encouragement.

Recently, the prison evangelists honored a "graduate" who had been released. She had paid her debt to society. Having learned of Christ while in the prison, she was baptized into Christ. Her Christian friends gave her an adequate wardrobe. They secured a job for her. They were crying and rejoicing! It was a moving occasion and one that we pray will be repeated a thousand times. This lady spoke with tears in her eyes and in her voice. She thanked her Christian friends for their gifts, and for finding her a job and a place to stay; but most of all she thanked them for giving themselves and for the love, care and concern they had shown. This local mission work results in 100 or more baptisms annually.

Personal Evangelism

The Madison Church carries on an active program of cottage meetings. It has several workers who have become very proficient in home cottage meetings. This specialized work calls for common sense, a knowledge of the scriptures, and a wonderful love for lost souls. When properly used, it is a blessing to the congregation.

Often, the program of benevolent work and teaching results in people wanting to become Christians. Qualified teachers assist them in understanding and completing their obedience.

It is important to enroll these prospects in a Bible class, and to keep them interested in church work. The personal evangelists should teach them the way of the Lord, and help keep their interest keen. One medical doctor baptized ten in one year and so cultivated and looked after the converts that each one was still faithful a year later.

The cottage meeting does not compete with other good programs. It is one way, among many, of sharing Christ. An active, wide awake congregation will use every means at its disposal to reach the lost and to keep Christians interested and serving the Lord.

10

BENEVOLENT WORK

The Bible has much to say about helping the poor, the lowly, the homeless, the helpless, the aged, the fatherless, and the widows. By studying the budget of the average church, it is easy to see that this is often the weakest area of church work. Frequently we simply do not "condescend to men of low estate" as is commended in Romans 12:16.

But we have discovered that wonderful, amazing, and unbelievable things happen to a church when it strives to practice, as well as preach, pure and undefiled religion!

The goal is to give 33 percent of the budget for benevolent work, 33 percent for mission work, and 33 percent for the teaching program at home.

In doing the work of the church there has to be imaginative plans, bold thinking, to accomplish anything good.

A church must be big enough to meet the needs of the members, and have a program of work and service covering many areas of concern. This is especially true of urban churches.

The church must become involved in people's lives or "it will become distant from people's lives, and thus useless to them."

*The church must become involved in
people's lives . . . .*

Child Care Program

Several years ago, the Madison church determined to
help take care of homeless children. It was told there
were over two million unloved, unwanted, neglected,
abandoned, abused, homeless boys and girls. At that
time, the membership could hardly believe it; today, it
does.

*There were over two million unloved,
unwanted, neglected, abandoned, abused,
homeless boys and girls.*

A committee of eleven men, full of faith and the Holy
Spirit, studied every child care program they could
find. They recommended building a normal-size home
and place a father, mother, and a maximum of six
children in each home.

When talk of this plan began, there was no money
and no land. Wonderful and glorious things happened
when we actually and sincerely determined to practice
pure and undefiled religion. A forty-two acre subdivision was acquired at a very low price. It was a marvelous
piece of land but still no money.

The decision to give all Sunday school classes an
opportunity to give a little extra for homeless, neglected
children was put into effect. The regular weekly contribution was not affected.

The elders and child care committee thought a small cottage plan would be more expensive, but they considered worth, not cost! God intended for every little boy and girl to have a father and mother. The finalized plan met that need.

Our aim is to provide a home that is best for the child. Practically all these children have varying degrees of emotional personality problems—unwanted, unloved, kicked-about, or shocked and bewildered by unhappy experiences. It is our purpose to provide a home that can supply the needs of these children. Every child deserves to grow up in a normal, Christian home.

Houseparents are selected by the child care committee and approved by the elders. The couple "must be faithful Christians, happily married, love children, and be happy, well-adjusted people." The house is furnished rent free with an allowance for each child.

There is no sign designating the homes in the subdivision. It appears to the public like other lovely homes. The children are not known as "orphan-home kids," but as Mr. and Mrs. Jones' foster children.

Such a home makes it possible for a child to feel that he is wanted, that he really has a father and mother, and of course, brothers and sisters. Each of our couples are able to take their families on trips in the family car, and go to church, town, or out to a restaurant, just as any other family.

There are now six beautiful brick homes (four bedrooms, two baths) each on one acre. The child care subdivision is called Happy Acres. A father and mother guide each home.

To the satisfaction of the group, the cost has been actually less per child. A child-care program in normal-size homes has been refreshing, successful, and wonderful.

Today, by the grace of God and the generosity of working people, the beautiful homes are paid for and filled with children. There are now three full time social workers directing and working in the adoptive and foster homes.

Because trained social workers are employed, there is offered a wide range of services: Children's Homes, Foster Home Care, Adoptive Services, Maternity Services for Unwed Mothers, and a Domestic Violence Program and Shelter.

One of the tremendous advantages of such a plan is that, instead of giving $25 a month for orphan children somewhere else, the Madison church is now giving almost $200,000 a year locally. Every time the church doors are open, these young parents and their "children" are present. When the fathers and mothers come into worship with the children, it is an eloquent sermon. They are some of the best dressed and the best behaved in the congregation.

When the fathers and mothers come into worship with the children, it is an eloquent sermon.

The state requires that Madison Children's Home have a Board of Directors. The Child Care Administrative Committee serves as that Board. The Elders and minister serve as the Board of Trustees. There is also a superintendent, one of the elders in keeping with Romans 13. A Director of Social Services with a Masters degree directs the work under the supervision of the Committee and Superintendent. The state has been very kind to the program and very appreciative of the work. They have worked closely with the program and know that these foster children receive much love and care.

It is thrilling to know many other congregations have built children's homes. Many have rented or bought a home in the middle of a block—put a young father, mother, and several children in this home. Several congregations have been so pleased with their first effort, they are now operating multiple units.

Congregations with a home for the local preacher might also consider at least one children's home.

We recently passed a milestone. Over 1000 children have been served by this program. We are grateful for having had the opportunity to touch their lives. Some of them are now married and sharing their own homes with the less fortunate.

Domestic Violence Shelter

Our newest service under the Children's Home umbrella is the Domestic Violence Program and Shelter. Statistics show that domestic violence occurs in a high percentage of homes, unfortunately including Christian homes. The Elders' first objective is rescue and safety, to save mothers' and children's lives; then, to assist mothers in whatever other decisions are necessary to insure safety and an adequate home life for themselves and their children. It is hoped these people in desperate need, will see Jesus in this work, and be drawn to Him and His church.

Furniture Warehouse

The men of Madison have a workshop and warehouse where they rebuild and store furniture and appliances for the less fortunate. Their slogan is printed on the sides of their pick-up truck—"Madison Church of Christ. Dealers in Faith, Hope and Charity." Each year, these retired men, through the furniture warehouse and workshop, help hundreds of families, averaging more than one per day. There are many thrilling stories regarding this work. Some have said that often, before the fire engine arrives, Madison's retired men are on the site offering help to the family.

"Madison Church of Christ. Dealers in Faith, Hope and Charity."

The entire benevolent program is evangelistic. The needy are helped first and questions asked later. The men who help always tell them that they, like the congregation, need Jesus. Many cottage Bible meetings have been held and many have been converted to Christ through the benevolent program.

It is amazing what doors of opportunity are opened by benevolent work. The church's reputation in the community as the people who care, is enhanced. It brings great blessings. Many congregations now have a workshop or warehouse where they rebuild and gather furniture to give to the poor and the needy—another way of practicing pure and undefiled religion.

Ladies' Sewing Group

Almost from its beginning the Madison church has had a sewing and quilting group.

The first group met once a month in private homes, making garments for children's homes, and piecing and making quilts.

As the program grew the elders designated a meeting place at the church building. Ladies began meeting and sewing five days a week. One day they quilt, the next day they knit, the next day they make dresses, etc. Several items are made especially for the shut-ins, and nursing home residents in the community. One night is designated for ladies who work outside the home. These ladies sew, and send greeting cards to the sick, shut-ins and bereaved.

Through the years there have been made a variety of garments: dresses, underwear, T-shirts, pants, shirts, pajamas, gowns, baby blankets, robes, hospital gowns, sheets, pillow cases, pillows, and gifts for nursing homes and shut-ins.

Ladies with small children, or who do not have transportation to the building, take supplies home, and make articles. This gives everyone an opportunity to contribute to the sewing program.

Occasionally special classes are offered to the members: smocking, sewing, needlepoint, etc. Saturday classes for young girls are also offered. This serves a two-fold purpose: creating better homemakers by learning a new skill; and making a contribution to the sewing program.

Not the least of the benefits of helping the needy is the great Christian fellowship these ladies enjoy.

Clothing Room

Madison's clothing room is open five days a week. Clothing is gathered, renovated, sized, and stocked for dispensing. A different team of Clothing Room ladies provide this service each weekday.

Only good clothing is given in the name of Jesus. People are asked to bring clothing that has been cleaned and is in good condition. New clothes are made from the many bolts of donated cloth. Tens of thousands of pieces of clothing have been given to the less fortunate.

Ladies' Knitting Group

The Ladies' Knitting Group began meeting during the late 1960's. They purposed to teach the craft for leisure enjoyment, while creating useful items for shut-ins and those in nursing homes.

Through the years, hundreds of items such as house shoes, bed jackets, lap robes, knee warmers, and scarves have been distributed to the nursing homes in the Nashville area, and to the shut-ins of the Madison church. Pea caps are knitted for our youngsters at the children's homes.

The fellowship of this group is a fulfilling and rewarding experience, and the items produced are useful and appreciated by the recipients.

Food Room

The food room is operated through the Benevolent office by volunteer personnel. The work is supervised by a retired deacon.

There are two major sources of food for this operation. Barrels prepared by our Art Department are placed in each Bible school department. Students are asked to bring food for the needy. In addition, on the first Sunday of each month, adults bring food which they deposit in containers, conveniently placed around the building. Much food is received from the warehouses of great chain stores. They contribute truck loads of food to the needy for distribution through the Madison program. A local Christian school donates a large quantity of food annually. These sources total about 85 percent of the needs to answer several hundred requests per month. The additional 15 percent is purchased by the church.

This office also handles all requests for financial aid.

Saturday Samaritans

The Saturday Samaritans were organized to preserve the homes of widows and others in need. They have a van to transport their equipment.

The Saturday Samaritans have various occupations, but one love in common. These Christian men volunteer their time and talent in several small crews. Each man works about two Saturdays each year of the physical and spiritual welfare of the people they are assisting. The Saturday Samaritans put James 1:27 into practice.

Home Health Care

Home Health Care was established to make visits to shut-ins who are not otherwise being seen on a regular basis by health care personnel. It is free to the congregation and for the congregation only. R.N.'s and L.P.N.'s give of their time to help in this ministry.

Transportation

Transportation is furnished for anyone needing to visit the doctor. Approximately 35 people volunteer one day each month as a driver, or substitute driver. The Madison community is helped and, upon request, the American Cancer Society uses the service for patients who are transported to radiation therapy.

Volunteer Sitters

The Volunteer Sitters program provides a needed service within the church. A group of men and women volunteer their time, individually, to stay with patients in the hospital day or night, relieving family members.

Another phase of this program provides sitters for shut-ins when relatives need to be away for short periods. Schedules are arranged to meet each family's needs.

Christian Care

Christian Care is a program to provide special care and housing for those in the sunset years of life. The goal is to provide this care in a Christian atmosphere at a reasonable cost.

Christian Care has brought great joy and happiness to the church members. It is relatively easy to get folks excited about helping little children. It is also important to help those who are older. Those who have seen their parents grow old know that in the golden years there are special problems. The need for Christian care, love and concern is great.

The program began in 1971 as the *Golden Age Village*

(Retirement Center), on property not far from the church building. An architect provided plans for twelve condominiums in clusters of three. There is a common courtyard and a fellowship and utilities room. Each home is completely private and designed especially to maintain independence in the golden years. Ten years later ten more cottages in clusters of five were built to the south of the original village. All are debt free and occupied by retired Christians who are a great credit to the church. Transportation where needed is furnished to all activities of the church. The Madison elders serve as the board of directors. The Christian Care Committee appointed by the elders administers the program. The Associates Committee plans activities for the village and sees that those in the golden years feel loved, wanted and accepted. The dream of the church is to have the facilities and personnel to address the total physical and spiritual needs of the aged. The young people are taught to respect and love older people, and to give attention and due consideration to them.

Ira and Avon North Retirement Center

The newest addition is an elegant villa completed in 1985 to provide independent living and supervised care for up to 24 residents in a congregate setting. Each resident has a private or semi-private bedroom furnished with his/her own furniture. Each has a private bath. Three meals a day are served in the attractive dining room adjacent to the beautifully furnished living room centered with a cozy fireplace. Home health-care services are provided for each resident. Weekly social activities are planned by the Volunteer Activities Director.

The cost of the building with furnishings was approximately $400,000.00, raised in a one-time special collection.

A program to serve the residents of Golden Age Village was created by a group of about ten women in November, 1970, and now serves the villa as well.

The Madison Church believes it has responsibilities in the care for each other as instructed in Holy Writ. While the natural family has primary responsibility to meet the needs of their own, often it is not possible for a family to provide all the needed care for their aged loved ones. As a Christian family, the church must not become insensitive, but provide for its own where necessary.

Serving the retirement center is a special committee whose main thrust is to be a "pal" on an individual basis to the residents. They are responsible to remember that individual as an occasional dinner guest for meals and on holidays and birthdays. They often furnish personal transportation. The committee sponsors monthly covered dish luncheons. Token dues are received from committee members for remembering residents in the hospital or in case of death.

This program provides much joy for the committee members and especially for the residents of the center—the villa and the residential condominium homes.

The Psalmist pled, "Cast me not off in the time of old age; forsake me not when my strength faileth." (Psalm 71:9) This is the continuing challenge in Christian Care.

Meals On Wheels

Meals on Wheels is a vital part of our benevolent program. Elderly citizens in the community who, because of ill health or financial problems, are not able to prepare one good balanced meal per day, are offered this service. The program is operated by volunteers. Several organize, some cook, and others deliver.

A government health nurse provides names of those who need this service. All local races, religions, or national origins are served in this program. Any human being is precious in the sight of God, and if in need is our neighbor.

Thousands of meals are served at very low cost to the church. Donations of food and money have come in to the program. Those who have participated report receiving great satisfaction and joy. Those we serve, often say: "Don't hurry, stay and visit a while." Often they request prayer.

Meals on wheels has brought the church respect and admiration of the community. It is an opportunity to help many who will never be able to do anything materially in return. The Bible teaches that this brings rewards from the Father in Heaven. It certainly has brought rewards to the Madison church.

It is an opportunity to help many who will never be able to do anything materially in return.

Sunshine Girls Visitation

Many vital parts of the Mission Program are on the local level. Each week, the Madison "Sunshine Girls" visit nursing and/or convalescent homes in the area. They give every patient a bud vase containing a fresh flower. Those who are able to sit up or walk often meet them in the hall, anxious for their visits!

Some of these patients have practically no other visitors. This program has brought hope, happiness, and joy to many lonely people. They learn to love the women who come, and look forward to their weekly visit. This visiting, in the name of Jesus, is an effective mission work and has blessed the church in many ways. The flowers are purchased reasonably through the courtesy of a local florist. Through this visitation program, many have been baptized and hundreds have experienced a warm and receptive feeling for the Lord's church.

11

WORSHIP AND PUBLIC ASSEMBLIES

The church believes it is important to obey the admonition, "do all things decently and in order."

Time . . . A Precious Commodity

The worship assemblies are orderly. Worship starts on time and ends on time. Some have objected to the adherence to a specific schedule, but objections have never been heard from shift workers, young mothers with several small children, or families who want to plan a day of fellowship, visitation or rest. Starting and stopping on the advertised time will do wonders for attendance, atmosphere, and public relations.

Starting and stopping on the advertised time will do wonders for attendance, atmosphere, and public relations.

Keeping a schedule demands advance planning and careful consideration to detail. Announcements (made while late arrivals enter the building), are kept to an absolute minimum. Those who serve as ushers and table servers, receive advance notice and are expected to be in place 10 minutes before worship. The song leader and preacher have designated time frames and they work together to use them in the most effective way. Sufficient time is allotted for baptisms or special announcements. Where this time is not needed, the song leader can be flexible. Exceptions to the allotted time arrangement are made only rarely.

To keep within these guidelines requires extra study by the preacher and good planning by the song leader, but it pays big dividends.

Worship Host

The elders have also learned the value of a host or coordinator for the public assemblies. Sometimes it is an elder or sometimes one of the ministers—but always someone is in charge. His objective is to keep the program moving, to have those assigned to read or pray, up, standing at the microphone and ready when asked. Dead spots are avoided and long delays are not a problem.

Handling Responses

When there are responses during a worship service, two groups react immediately. An usher hands the respondee a card and pencil and assists in gathering the information. In the event of a baptism, someone accompanies the candidate to a dressing room and assists in every way possible.

If the responder, usually with a tender and emotional heart, wishes to confess public error or requests prayer of the congregation, an elder, previously designated, assists the individual and encourages him or her in whatever way possible. This not only makes the responder more comfortable, it says to the congregation that the elders are shepherding the flock, interested, and ready to help.

The Contribution

In the event of a baptism, ushers take the weekly collection while preparation is made for the baptism. Again, time is used efficiently, and order is preserved.

A worship in spirit and in truth must be edifying as well as reverent. Organization will make water run uphill. The members will appreciate the efficiency and the visitors will be impressed with the effort to do things right.

Communion Preparation

When 3,000 are to be served, communion preparation requires advanced thought. At the same time, the church strives hard to preserve reverence and authenticity. It takes no longer to serve 3,000 (about 9 minutes) than it takes most congregations to serve 200. The secret is prayerful preparation and orderly execution.

"Home made" bread is provided by volunteers who bake it on monthly schedules. All the young girls are taught to make the communion loaf.

The communion trays are cleaned and polished regularly. They are prepared and placed in position by one of the staff. This staffer also assists those who need portable communion facilities for outside visitation.

Worship In Song

The elders strongly urge congregations to use only their very best song leader at all public assemblies.

When the song leader directs in an unorganized, haphazard way, the result will be poor singing and ineffective worship. When different song leaders rotate the duties, the congregation learns to follow no one.

At Madison the singing sets the mood for the entire worship. The professionally trained song leader and designated back-up, give serious advanced thought to the selection and direction of the worship in song.

At Madison the singing sets the mood for the entire worship.

The elders believe it is important to have the very best classroom teachers, the very best pulpit speakers, and the very best song leaders available. This is one of the greatest advantages of a large congregation. The talent and means is immense. We seek to use them to God's advantage.

12

BUSINESS AFFAIRS

With so many programs and a 25 member, full time church staff, it is absolutely necessary that Madison conduct its work in a businesslike manner. Any church which plans to grow must discipline itself to keep good records, maintain proper communication between the workers, and budget itself through the resources and faith to meet the demands of tomorrow.

Business Office

The Business Office (open five days a week) keeps track of all contributions and expenditures. Each department's budget is monitored. Weekly and monthly reports are available to the elders. When large amounts of money are awaiting expenditure, they are carefully invested, so they might work for the Lord while awaiting designated use.

Accounting

Eight accounts are maintained for business purposes, each computerized for accurate record keeping. The regular church account is used for routine church business and payroll. The Madison Children's Home account is used to pay four full-time employees in that department; Valley View, the summer camping program has 24 employees; The Christian Care Center has seven employees; Christian Productions Inc. maintains accounts for the purchase of all advertising; pays three full-time employees, and handles expenses for the Amazing Grace Bible Class; the Tuesday/Thursday School has 32 employees, and Bible Kindergarten, six, thus making it wise to maintain a separate account for each of these. Finally the Madison Missions program with its eight full time employees has a separate account to maintain the needs of each of these programs including missionaries. These accounts pay all bills and salaries, and maintain all records for a total of 109 employees.

Employee Records

Employee records are confidential and employees are well informed as to the status of their salary and benefits. A program of health and retirement benefits is available to all paid personnel.

Bills are paid on time.

Communication with missionaries is carefully maintained to prevent personal emergency. Equipment records, such as warranties and maintenance records, are methodically stored for recall.

Keeping such a vast collection of records and working budgets is simplified greatly by the use of a computer. The six station, mainframe computer contains all membership records as well as business records. Access to this information is by special permission through the Eldership.

Two letter quality printers give the various offices

access to word processing. This greatly simplifies correspondence, weekly chores such as schedules, publications, etc., and keeps mailing lists current and accurate.

The elders believe the church owes its members accurate accountability in business matters and faithful attention to all that involves the financial sacrifices of its supporters. The computerization of church records and secretarial services are recommended, especially for the larger congregations.

13

THE PRICELESS INGREDIENT

The "ceiling unlimited" attitude, hard work, and "keeping the unity of the spirit in the bond of peace," are everyday concepts at Madison. By the grace of God and constant prayer, they have been able to do just that.

Often a delicate situation requires great patience and prayer. One of the bishops puts this philosophy into words. He says, "Authority is like money in the bank—the less you use it, the more you have."

There are occasions that require great tact as well as patience and prayer. The elders are not quick to withdraw fellowship to or call someone "on the carpet." However, when the circumstances demand, they do make such decisions—definitely, emphatically, and clearly. In doing so they follow the direction of scripture explicitly.

The membership cooperates with the elders by following their leadership. The shepherds through their patience, courage, faith, and prayer, have the complete confidence of their fellow Christians. They have earned our respect and admiration.

"The Unity Of The Spirit In The Bond Of Peace"

The church in Jerusalem had a great benevolent program. The church in Jerusalem, the model church for all ages, had a great educational program. The church of our Lord in Jerusalem had a great mission program. Yet this is not the entire story. These great programs existed in the framework of unity of the spirit in the bond of peace.

As a people we speak with great eloquence on unity. We memorize the appropriate passages. All too often they are applied to other religious groups and not often enough to the Lord's church. These great passages on unity apply to every member, every congregation.

What does it profit to have a great educational program, a wonderful benevolent program, and a fine mission program, only to be blown sky high with a church fuss?

Many congregations have a bright future. The church is growing. The people of the community are learning to love, appreciate and respect the church. Then comes the church fuss. That ends the growth and the hope of a great church.

A church fuss sometimes takes several generations to heal. Madison has been extremely fortunate. Since the beginning, it has not known a division. There has never been a church fuss.

A church fuss sometimes takes several generations to heal.

That priceless ingredient . . . "the unity of the spirit in the bond of peace ". . . is Madison's trademark! We endeavor to fly it like a flag! The members are committed to getting along, to loving one another, to forgiving one another, to boosting one another, and to each esteeming the other better than himself. The "unity of the spirit in the bond of peace" must be kept if we want the church to grow.

"the unity of the spirit in the bond of peace ". . . is Madison's trademark!

How Do You Keep It?

Madison Church does not claim to have all the answers. The membership works at it every day, seven days a week, 365 days a year.

They are committed to having the Lord's Supper on the Lord's Day because the Bible commands it. They are committed to immersion for remission of sins because the Bible commands it. They are committed to singing because the Bible commands it. The members are committed to keeping the "unity of the spirit in the bond of peace" because the Bible commands it.

Prayers for unity are offered every day, in every service, in every meeting, constantly and urgently. The membership begs for the wisdom that comes from above, that is first peaceable. No one has the wisdom to motivate thousands to work together in unity and love without the help of God the Father.

Unity Starts At The Top

Unity begins at the top. The elders and ministers must set an example. It is the policy of this congregation for "each to esteem the other better than himself." Everyone has his say, but no one has his way, all the time. There is no dictatorship. The elders do not believe in one man or minority rule. In expedient matters when the majority of the pastors say go, then the minority cooperates. In matters of faith and principle, they have always been one.

This policy is priceless and essential in the operation of a great church. Often the trouble in local congregations is over matters of judgment and expediency. When a congregation chooses sides on anything, there is trouble. If it becomes "us and them", the congregation is in trouble. Everybody is loved at Madison; however, they do not want and will not welcome or tolerate any person who causes trouble or divides the body of Christ. There are many precious children depending on the members. There are many missionaries who need support—there are many opportunities to spread the gospel of Christ—we have many poor, lowly, downtrodden, and lonely who need love and assistance. Energy must not be spent fussing, fighting, or talking ugly about one another. Every person's energy must be used in the cause of Christ.

The Love Feast And Spirit Of Concern

A great aid in promoting unity is the spirit of friendliness and love exhibited during the public assemblies. They are extremely anxious for everyone attending the services at Madison to feel wanted and appreciated. Coldness, formality and a ritualistic atmosphere do not produce growth. To help cultivate friendliness, there is a corps of ushers. They open doors and shake hands with everyone attending.

Before every service the membership takes 60 seconds for a "love feast." The entire audience stands and shakes hands with those around them. Each one introduces himself and says something nice. "If you cannot love your fellowman whom you have seen, how can you love God whom you haven't seen?" People are reminded that it is reverent, godly, and wonderful to see members of the Lord's church shaking hands and expressing love, care and concern. This sixty second love feast has been an effectual part of the growth of the Madison Church.

The entire audience stands and shakes hands with those around them. Each one introduces himself and says something nice.

At the close of every service couples are placed at each door to warmly shake hands with everyone who leaves, reminding them of the joy in having them. It takes a lot of people to accomplish this task and the elders strive to use someone different at every service. This also serves another great purpose. It gives the members recognition and helps them to know one another better. Each of the members wears a name tag. This helps overcome recognition problems.

"Especially Those Of The Household Of Faith"

At Madison the leadership is sensitive to need. They are not hesitant to pass the basket an extra time. On many occasions, members have given extra to help some family in time of crisis. This has not affected the regular contribution. It has, in fact, helped it.

The members at Madison give their money, their hearts, their time and talents to the work of the Lord. In times of tragedy, trouble or old age, the members stand by, ready to help. God grant that it may ever be so!

Neighborhood Groups

It has often been asked, "How do you look after almost 5,000 individuals?"

This is accomplished by keeping emphasis on the individual. One soul is worth more than all the world. Jesus spoke of leaving the ninety-nine and going after the one. It is that one more that keeps the church striving. Each individual Christian has a responsibility as his brother's keeper.

Paul says, "Bear ye one another's burdens." To carry out this Biblical admonition, Madison is divided into geographical areas, guided by an elder and usually assisted by husband-and-wife teams, designated by the elders. Each area includes approximately twelve families. When individuals are baptized into Christ, or place membership, they are assigned to one of these groups. These families meet in homes for meals and fellowship. All group leaders, area leaders, and elders, are striving to know everyone in their area on a personal basis. All members working with their group leaders have these obligations:

1. Attend all meetings of the group.
2. Report any new people in the zone, visit them and welcome them to Bible Study and worship.
3. Report to the church office any family moving away and where they are moving.
4. Report and visit the sick in your zone. Offer help when needed.
5. Report death and visit bereaved. Assist when possible.
6. Report the arrival of a new baby.
7. Report good prospects to personal evangelism team.
8. Visit, encourage, and invite those who are irregular in attendance.
9. Help distribute advertising material.
10. Assist in getting new members involved in local work.

Crisis and Criticism

Another question often asked . . . . does Madison have any problems? The answer, of course, is yes. It does have problems. There have been crises and heartbreaks, as will any growing congregation. However, you don't build by emphasizing the negative.

You don't build by emphasizing the negative.

When a department or program at Madison begins to get negative in any way, that department is beginning to die. You do not build a happy home by emphasizing your partner's faults. Every effort is made to keep the program positive. The people are trained to think and act positively. Should a program cease to have a positive influence, it is discontinued.

When crises come, they need to be met boldly, courageously and swiftly, yet with fairness and tact and great wisdom. The church policy with clashes of personalities and matters of expediency is to exercise great patience, faith, and prayer. Most of these problems will solve themselves if those attributes are practiced.

In problems where there is sin or where moral principles are at stake, it is the policy of the leaders at Madison to act courageously, boldly, and with dispatch.

"Operation Forward"—Planning Ahead With Faith And Vision

For many years the Madison Church has had an annual planning session. The elders admonished us, "always plan more than you can do by yourselves," always leave room for God to help.

The membership understands the importance of business planning. This principle applies also in church work. At Madison, this process is called Operation Forward.

Often a state park or lodge is rented away from the hustle and bustle of city life and a day is spent in planning. Usually the elders and ministers go on Friday night and talk about the work of the Lord. The deacons and Bible school leaders, zone leaders, and key people come the next day for planning.

Prior to Operation Forward, the congregation is asked to submit ideas for growth and special programs. These ideas are also considered and expanded during Operation Forward.

No decisions are made in these sessions. The

members talk. The elders listen. The session lasts the entire day and into the night.

The child care program, Bible kindergarten, television ministry, Bible camp, and many other programs, were first suggested by some dedicated person at these planning sessions.

Time is given for anyone to propose any idea for the advancement of the cause of Christ. The elders, in private, weigh those ideas and ask the questions: Is it scriptural? Is it practical? Is it right? Will it please the Lord? Will it advance the Kingdom of God on earth?

Is it scriptural? Is it practical?
Is it right? Will it please the Lord? Will
it advance the Kingdom of God on earth?

SUMMARY

The Madison church has a rich heritage and a bright future. It has determined to continue sowing the seeds of undenominational Christianity. It strives daily to represent Christ in the community. It looks forward to His second coming.

It looks forward to His second coming.

It is the sincere prayer of the Madison leadership and its members that this book will boost the work of God's Kingdom worldwide, and that many will come to know God's saving grace through the influence of strong, active local congregations of Christ's church, busying themselves in His vineyard.

Madison Milestones

	August-Sept.	
1934	November	Home meetings to discuss congregation establishment. Canvassed door to door.
	December	First worship of Madison Church of Christ. Thirteen month lease signed, $15.00 per month.
1935	May	Building committee appointed.
	June	Lot on Gallatin Road (83 x 102) donated by Miss Opha Bixler.
	August	First promotional advertising giveaway for a Gospel meeting.
	November	Trustees appointed: Dr. M. A. Beasley, A. K. Buchser, S. L. Lillie, G. L. Campbell and H. B. McPherson.
	December	Building note for $5,500 signed at Madison Bank.
1936	January	First meeting in "Little Rock Chapel".
	August	First full time minister, L. Haven Miller, hired. First Elders appointed: Dr. M. A. Beasley, H. B. McPherson and J. L. Hunter. First Deacons appointed: G. L. Campbell, S. S. Lowe, Jr., S. L. Lillie, T. J. Ladd, and James Cox.
	September	First church directory published.

1937	June	Tent meeting with S. H. Hall and Joseph McPherson resulted in additions. S. L. Lillie appointed elder. Dave C. Slaughter installed as deacon.
1938	June	Elders and deacons wrote an open letter stating that the "CHURCH IS AGAINST BEER GARDENS, DANCE HALLS, ROAD HOUSES AND SUNDAY MOVIES THAT CONTRIBUTE TO THE BREAKDOWN OF THE MORALS OF THE PEOPLE."
1939	October	First Gospel meeting in the church building, membership reaches 195.
1940	April	Harris J. Dark replaces L. Haven Miller as local preacher.
1941	January	GOSPEL ECHO, first church paper, published. First church budget—$100.00 weekly.
	November	EVENING BIBLE COLLEGE & TRAINING SCHOOL. Classes in Bible subjects and Greek for children and adults.
1942	December	Mission program expanded to include W. W. Littlejohn and J. P. Galloway.
1944	January	C. J. Garner replaced Harris J. Dark as local preacher. GOSPEL WORKER, new bulletin published by C. J. Garner.
1945	February	Printing Press purchased; pictures, tracts and illustrations printed.
	March	Sunday School Attendance Drive Motto: LET'S MAKE IT 400 BY MAY 1ST.
	May	Attendance Over the Top—446.
	September	Bulletin hand delivered to every

101

		home announced Gospel meeting.
	October	Additional property purchased from Opha Bixler. Expansion plans pushed.
1946	January	First phase construction for basement auditorium
1947	February	First effort at zoning. Sixteen zones outlined. Religious census estimates 700 members in area.
	July	First service in new basement auditorium, 497 present.
1948	January	New men's training class begun.
1949	March	Juvenile Court Judge Sam Davis Tatum, speaks on BIBLE SCHOOL ATTENDANCE. Used Army bus purchased for $900.00. Ernest Chilton, driver.
	December	Madison #2 in Bible Study attendance in Davidson County.
1950	January	New annual budget $31,290.00.
	May	Sunday School Drive Success— 742 present.
1951	January	New Elders appointed: S. H. Litton and W. H. Roark.
	May	May 20th Sunday School Drive. 1,000 expected, 1,170 attended. OVER THE TOP.
1952	January	Lester F. Frawley interim preacher.
	July	Ira North agreed to begin work October 1st.
	October	Special Building Fund for October 5th coinciding with first service with Ira North.
	November	GOSPEL WORKER changed to CHRISTIAN CALLER.
1953	January	Goals for New Year: Bible School 700, Worship 900, all in new building.
1954	October	New zoning program begun with 39 geographical areas.

		Alvin Dunkleberger appointed elder.
1955	April	Additional morning service begun.
	May	Bible Correspondence School started, J. L. Hunter, director. Church Library begun with Otto Prater, Martha Batey and J. L. Hunter.
	October	First broadcast on WKDA radio of young people's class from Madison Fire Hall.
1956	February	Willard Collins guest speaker.
	April	Sunday School goal of 3,000 surpassed by two.
	June	Claude Lewis employed as Educational Director and Song Leader.
	August-Sept.	Four sessions of Bible camp at Short Mountain.
1957	December	OPERATION FORWARD first annual planning session.
1958	January	Extension Department begun, Roy Holt, Supervisor.
1959	January	Clayton Pepper employed as Court Evangelist for Juvenile Court.
	September	AWAY FROM HOME department begins. Ira North spoke to organizational rally to establish Ohio Valley Christian College.
	May	MADISON CHILDREN'S HOME chartered by the State Welfare Department.
	December	Charles Nelson appointed song leader.
1960	April	Groundbreaking for three cottages at HAPPY ACRES.
	September	HAPPY ACRES operation begun.
	November	Marquee erected, first slogan: "And Be Ye Thankful . . ."
1961	January	Old Lumber Company Building

		rented for Young People's Annex.
	July	"Five Golden Minutes" begun on WSIX-TV.
1962	September	MADISON BIBLE KINDERGARTEN begun, Marydee Holleman, Supervisor.
1963	September	$4,474.00 raised for debt retirement.
1964	January	Sunday School Annex completed.
	May	Congregation worshipped at Ryman Auditorium. $350,000.00 in construction bonds issued in 10 minutes.
1965	May	4,394 attended Sunday School. Second bond issue of $400,000.00 raised.
	November	LITTLE ANGELS BIBLE CLASS for retarded children begun. Maxine Sadler, Supervisor.
1966	April	New 3,000 seat auditorium opened.
	June	David Hearn to Madison.
	September	THURSDAY SCHOOL for pre-school children begun. Jo Anne North, Supervisor.
1967	April	MADISON WORKSHOPS begun, sharing programs and study ideas nationwide. Avon North, Supervisor.
1968	August	Charles R. Brewer became Assistant Minister.
	September	SUNSHINE GIRLS began visitation in nursing homes. Mrs. J. B. Stacey, Supervisor.
	October	Bus Ministry begun. The Gospel rolls along.
1969	January	Madison received Guidepost Church Award, presented by Dr. Norman Vincent Peale.
	May	Golden Age Village groundbreaking.
	June	Ben Jones named Youth Minister.

1970	April	Open House at Golden Age Village.
	May	Meals On Wheels begun. Avon North, Supervisor.
1971	February	Jerry Sherrill became Assistant Minister.
	June	Television's Amazing Grace Bible Class begun.
	October	Harold G. Cox appointed Prison Ministry Supervisor.
	December	Bill Ruhl appointed Associate Minister.
1973	April	Care N' Share Center renovated.
1974	May	Treasure Hunt-Egg Hunt and Sunday School picnic at Avondale Farm.
1975	January	Mr. & Mrs. R. C. Walker assumed direction of Bible Correspondence School.
	July	A. O. Stinson appointed Syndicator of Amazing Grace.
1976	January	Buck Dozier appointed Youth Director.
1977	January	Annual Budget $1,000,000.00.
	August	Family Life and Sunday School Annex expansion proposed.
	November	$250,000.00 collection goal—$462,400.00 received.
1978	January	Elder Howard Roberts, assumed fulltime position as Business Manager. Nick Boone employed as Child Care Director and Song Leader.
	June	Six elders appointed: Tom Brown, Clayton Gholson, Harold Gore, Charles Link, Bobby McElhiney, and George Terry.
	August	Cecil Wright added to staff for writing and research.
1979	June	J. M. Mankin and Bruce White began work as Associate Ministers.
	August	Seventy new deacons added.

1980	May	George Goldtrap, new Executive Producer of Amazing Grace.
	August	Groundbreaking for Christian Care Retirement Cottages.
	October	Twentieth Anniversary for Child Care.
1981	November	Ira North announced retirement from Gospel Advocate to devote fulltime to local ministry.
1982	May	Great Day in May Sunday School goal 8,000 attendance 8,410, with worship over 17,000.
	October	Norman Slate becomes Director of Personal Evangelism.
1983	September	1,000th child presented accomplishing 23 years of child care service.
1984	January	Ira North crossed Jordan; Jim Mankin appointed pulpit minister.
	March	600th Amazing Grace Program taped.
	October	Randolph Dunn and Bobby Hudson became 23rd and 24th elders in 50 year history.
	December	Open House at Ira and Avon North Christian Care Retirement Center.
1985	February	700th Amazing Grace Program taped.
	May	Dwight Sowle appointed Youth Minister. Buck Dozier appointed Family Life Minister.
	November	Combined Bible Study and Worship at Opry House, Opryland, USA.
1986	January	Domestic Violence Shelter started.
	February	New classroom construction started.
	April	Amazing Grace began satellite distribution.
	September	R. C. and Elizabeth Walker

	retire as directors of Bible Correspondence School. George Goldtrap named new director.
October	Jim Mankin announces plans to accept position with ACU effective January 1, 1987.
November	Grand Opening—three story educational building. Special contribution of $300,000.00. Jim Mankin's last Sunday. Twenty-three new deacons ordained, bringing total to over 200. Steve Flatt named pulpit minister.